Selected and transcribed by
GORDON SAUNDERS

EIGHT
TRADITIONAL
JAPANESE PIECES

FOR SOLO TENOR RECORDER,
DESCANT RECORDER OR FLUTE

Novello Publishing Limited

Contents

Introduction

The eight pieces, presented in order of difficulty, have been selected from the traditional folk music of Japan and represent the highly attractive song, dance and instrumental styles of that musically rich country. All these pieces would commonly be played on the Japanese 'shakuhachi', which is an end-blown flute of similar pitch and size to the tenor recorder and not without tonal relationships with that instrument. This book is primarily designed for the tenor recorder player and will fill, I hope, a long-existing lack of solo material for this most expressive member of the recorder family. Whilst many recorder players will wish only to use this selection as recreational pieces, they are fully suitable for concert performance and will receive, I feel sure, a pleasing audience response. In addition, they will offer, I fancy, a fair measure of satisfaction for the descant recorder player and the flautist, both of whom might well like to probe a style of music out of the ordinary run of available material.

Each piece has been given its authentic setting of introduction and ornamentation and such is the shared base of Japanese and Western music, that the player will rapidly establish confidence in the new medium. Indeed, the only innovation required may well be a more excessive form of breath pressure control than is usual in classical Western music and this will follow naturally after a little experimentation. In fact the main delight to be found in the eight works, is the opportunity to give free rein to staccato, variations in breath pressure from very low to the highest the instrument will take, and flexibility in tempo.

Editing has been completed with the modern recorder symbols as below:

- V   breath
- ᐯ   extra breath
- (V)   optional breath
- ,   break, aided by articulation
- ⌐‾‾‾‾⌐   echo effect

GORDON SAUNDERS

1 OWASE MELODY

OWASE BUSHI

2 PEASANTS' SONG

TOSA NO SUNAYAMA

INTRODUCTION
Serioso e molto espressivo ♩ = 56

3 ECHÛOHARA AIR

ECHÛOHARA – BUSHI

4 SANKAI MELODY

SANKI BUSHI

INTRODUCTION (Played normally)

Affettuoso ♩ = 66

This piece is to be played 'Shakuhachi' style*

mf — *mf* — *mf*   dim.   *pp* *vibrato throughout*

slow

f

The A is blown with increasing
volume over its (♩.) length.

*Hold the recorder almost perpendicular and blow
across the open end of the mouthpiece, as if sounding
a note from a milk bottle, with the lower lip firmly
placed against the mouthpiece, thus:

5 MOGAMI FERRYMAN'S SONG

MOGAMIGAWA FUNA-UTA

6 SAKURÁ

SAKURÁ

THEME
Lento con amore ♩ = 80

VARIATION I
♩ = 88
con brio

allargando

VARIATION II
♩ = 88
ritmico

rall.

VARIATION III
♩ = 80
cantabile   *simile*

allargando   *rall.*

vibrato

*B♭ to D trill — thumb and index finger (left hand) simultaneously

10

7 HAKATA AIR

HAKATA BUSHI

8 HORSEWALKER'S SONG

ESASHI OIWAKE

1/10 (172900)